Inside Meaning
Teacher's Book

Inside Meaning

Proficiency reading comprehension

Teacher's book

Michael Swan

CAMBRIDGE
UNIVERSITY PRESS

Published by the Press Syndicate of the University of Cambridge
The Pitt Building, Trumpington Street, Cambridge CB2 1RP
40 West 20th Street, New York, NY 10011-4211, USA
10 Stamford Road, Oakleigh, Victoria 3166, Australia

© Cambridge University Press 1978

First published 1978
Eighth printing 1992

Printed in Great Britain by
GreenShires Print Ltd, Kettering, Northamptonshire

ISBN 0 521 22132 3 Teacher's Book
ISBN 0 521 20972 2 Student's Book
ISBN 0 521 26347 6 Set of 2 cassettes

Contents

Contents

Contents

Section C: Perception of the effective use of English

Teaching unit 8: Appreciation of a writer's use of language 1   35

Teaching unit 9: Appreciation of a writer's use of language 2   39

Section D: Practice tests

Contents

Introduction

The teacher's book for *Inside Meaning* contains notes on the
texts, answers to the questions in the student's book, ideas for
speaking and writing exercises, and suggestions for using the
cassettes which accompany the book. Throughout the notes the
page-references given in brackets indicate pages of the student's
book; there are also cross-references to pages within the teacher's
book and these are followed by 'above' or 'below'.

Notes on the texts

Very brief notes are provided in order to supply information
about the authors, contexts or cultural background of some of
the passages, where this seems desirable.

Answers to the questions

The multiple-choice questions in *Inside Meaning* are intended to
have only one right answer in each case, and a student who
chooses an alternative different from the one shown here has
probably misunderstood either the text or the question. (In cases
where more than one answer does seem possible, this is shown
in brackets.) Other kinds of question, however, do not usually
have one 'right answer'. Differences of interpretation and
emphasis are often possible (especially in complex exercises like
summary-writing), and even where an answer seems straight-
forward it can generally be expressed in more than one way.

The answers should not, therefore, be regarded as 'model
answers'. They are simply one person's solutions to the problems;
teachers who have time to do the exercises themselves will easily
find other (and often better) formulations.

There is another reason for not treating these answers as
'models'. It is that they set an unrealistic linguistic standard for
the average foreign student. It can be very discouraging for a
learner to do a good piece of work, making intelligent use of all
the English he has at his command, and then to be shown something clearer and more elegant written by a fluent native speaker
with a much larger vocabulary. The answers, then (particularly

1

the summaries), should perhaps be used with discretion, and are probably best seen as an aid to the teacher rather than as a set of models to be held up for the struggling student to aspire to.

Suggestions for follow-up work

Most of the texts can obviously be used for other purposes besides pure comprehension practice. Suggestions are given for composition and discussion exercises related to the majority of the texts (not all of them are suitable for this kind of work, of course).

General methodological suggestions about how texts can be exploited for vocabulary study, composition and discussion will be found in the 'Notes for teachers' at the beginning of the student's book. It is perhaps worth re-emphasising here that, in language-teaching, you can only get out what you have already put in. In other words, a student can only be expected to write a good free composition, or to produce acceptable English in a discussion, if he already knows the structures, words and expressions appropriate to the subject. A very good student may already be in this position; others need to learn the necessary language as part of their preparation for the composition or discussion, and if they do not have this preparation they are likely to produce poor, disorganised work, full of mistakes and literal translations from the mother-tongue. It is therefore advisable, with most students, to do *input* work (vocabulary study and/or semi-controlled composition) on a particular text before going on to *output* work (free composition, discussion or role-playing).

The distinction between semi-controlled composition and free composition is important. In a semi-controlled composition, a student is asked to include certain of the most useful words and expressions (and perhaps structures) which he has learnt from the text. In using these new language items to express his own ideas, the student fixes them in his mind so that they are learnt effectively and will be available for use when he needs them. This kind of composition is a learning activity: the student knows more English when he has finished it than when he started. It is a powerful language-teaching tool, particularly with weaker students, and it makes an excellent preparation for discussion work (especially if the words and expressions to be used in the composition are chosen with the discussion subject in mind).

In a free composition, on the other hand, a student simply practises using the language he knows already, without learning anything new. This sort of fluency practice is valuable for very advanced students, and has the advantage that the writer is completely free to express his own ideas. However, it can be a discouraging exercise for a weaker student, who finds himself asked to say things he doesn't know how to say, and is therefore forced to 'invent' English, with the inevitable result that he makes large numbers of mistakes.

Most of the writing topics given here are semi-controlled compositions, but teachers who prefer to set free compositions need only give the subject to the students without telling them to include particular words or expressions from the text. The discussion subjects can also be done as free composition if preferred.

Using the cassettes

The texts listed below are recorded on cassette. These recordings can be exploited in various ways; the following suggestions may be helpful to teachers who wish to make use of them.

1. *Global listening comprehension.* Instead of using a text for reading comprehension practice, it can be used for training in listening. The simplest approach is to play the recording straight through from beginning to end and ask students to say what they have understood. Things can be made easier for the students by breaking the text into two or three sections, or by playing the recording more than once. Their attention can be focussed on particular points by asking specific questions; students who find this kind of exercise difficult can be helped to structure their listening by being given the questions in advance. If questions are answered orally, there is a danger that the students who need the practice most will participate least, so it may be advisable to have at least some of the questions answered in writing. The questions in the student's book may in some cases prove useful for listening work, but as they are designed for reading comprehension, not all of them will be suitable.

2. *Detailed listening comprehension.* The basic listening problem, for most students, is that the words seem to go by too fast. Part of the reason for this difficulty in 'catching' words is unfamiliarity with their pronunciation in sentences: it is often the simplest words (prepositions, auxiliary verbs, etc.) which are not understood. (This is usually because, in unstressed words, vowels and consonants are reduced or elided.) A good way of getting over this difficulty is by listening intensively to single sentences repeated several times, and trying to write or say every word that comes in the sentence. Teachers who want to do this kind of work should pick out sentences that contain no vocabulary

problems, but which have plenty of words with 'weak' pronunciations.

3. *Initial presentation of a text.* If a text is going to be used for language study rather than reading comprehension work, it can be more interesting to start with an oral presentation. The recording can be played either before the students see the text, or while they follow it in their books. Students often find it easier to concentrate on a text which is presented orally.

4. *Pronunciation.* The recordings can be used to familiarise students with different accents (they include examples of several different British and American pronunciations). Selected recordings can serve as models of pronunciation.

Recorded texts

Introduction

Section A:
Basic reading technique and multiple-choice tests

Teaching unit 1: How to read a text

Graduates

Answers to exercise a (page 8)

1 Changes in the British attitude to university education.
2 Yes.
3 That Britain had fewer universities, in proportion to her population, than almost any other civilised European country.
4 Fewer.
5 Fewer.
6 Not quite clear from the text – probably more.
7 A sceptical, indifferent or hostile attitude.
8 Yes.

Answers to exercise b (page 8)

1D.   2S? (perhaps Britain and Turkey had the same proportion of universities).   3S.   4D (the survey was not carried out by the Ministry of Education).   5S.   6S.
7D.   8S.   9S.   10D.

Follow-up work

Semi-controlled composition: Compare the university situation in Britain with that in your country.
Class discussion: Should university entrance be made more or less competitive?

The Hollywood Indian

Note on the text

Raymond Chandler wrote tough complicated thrillers set in California. His hero (the narrator in this text) is a private detec-

6

tive called Philip Marlowe. Later in the story, Marlowe and the Indian have a fight (hinted at in lines 15–16). Chandler has a very individual style, characterised by extravagant imagery and the frequent use of implication rather than direct statement.

Answers to exercise c (page 10)

1   Standing quite still (like a statue).
2   He had short legs.
3   His trousers were too long for him; they came up to his chest.
4   He wore it right on the top of his head.
5   It fitted very loosely.
6   They weren't awkward: he was very agile.
7   Making no noise.
8   They were already very wide.
9   It was stained with sweat.
10 He didn't look at all nervous.

Practice unit 1.1

Barbara's father

Answers to exercise a (page 11)

1b.   2c (or a).   3a.   4b.   5c.   6d (or b or a).
7d.   8b.   9d.   10d.

The Milestone Buttress

Note on the text

In the book from which this is taken, Eric Newby describes how he and a friend went to a remote part of Afghanistan and nearly succeeded in reaching the top of an unclimbed mountain (Mir Samir). Their only experience of climbing came from a few days' lessons in North Wales – the first lesson is described here.

Answers to exercise b (page 13)

1a.   2c.   3a.   4c.   5c.   6b.   7b.   8d.
9c.   10b.

Follow-up work

Talks, by any members of the class who have done rock-climbing, about their experiences.

Practice unit 1.2

The bomb

Note on the text

Adam Hall writes spy thrillers involving a character called Quiller. This one is set in Berlin. Hall enjoys giving lots of technical details (see lines 24–30) — this can make him difficult to read.

Answers to exercise a (page 16)

1S.	2S.	3D.	4S.	5D.	6S.	7D.	8D.
9S.	10S.						

A level chemistry

Answers to exercise b (page 17)

1b.	2d.	3c.	4a.	5d.	6b.	7a.	8b.
9c.	10c.						

Follow-up work

Semi-controlled composition: What do you think of this teacher's attitude to education? How does it compare with the approach in your own school?
Class discussion on same subject.

This text could be studied in combination with 'Adolescent students' (page 63), 'Education, a father's experience' (page 61) and/or 'Grammar school' (page 132).

Practice unit 1.3

⬛ **I re-run the replica hijack**

Answers to exercise (page 19)

1b.   2d.   3a (or d).   4a.   5d.   6b.   7c.
8d.   9b.   10b.   11b.   12a.   13a.   14c.
15d.   16c.

Teaching unit 2: Guessing unknown words

Answers to exercise a (page 22)

1   clumsy.
2   bad-mannered.
3   small hill.
4   sticky; between liquid and solid.
5   walking with feet dragging on the ground.
6   special kind of paint put on under ordinary paint.
7   miserable, sad.
8   small cuts in wood.
9   ring of rubber or other material used to make a metal
     joint waterproof.
10   ready to believe anything one's told.

Drumming

Note on the text

This is an extract from an interview with a burglar. Most of the
words in italics are either cockney or thieves' slang; *pushover,
narrow squeaks* and *pinched* are slangy colloquial English.

Answers to exercise b (page 22)

drumming: burgling empty houses.
dead gaff: empty house.
turn the place over: search the house for things to steal.
a pushover: very easy.
drummer: this kind of burglar.
take stoppo: escape.
two-handed team: team of two.
nicked: caught.
grafted: worked.
narrow squeaks: narrow escapes.
pinched: caught.
manor: district.

Practice unit 2.1

Hamburgers and Hamlet

Answers to exercise a (page 24)

1b.   2a.   3c.   4c.   5a.   6b.   7a.   8a.
9c.   10c.   11d.   12c.

Follow-up work

Semi-controlled composition: Write about a tourist centre in your country which has the same sort of problems as Stratford.

A car chase

Note on the text

This is taken from one of Fleming's well-known stories about the British secret agent James Bond. Drax and Krebs are, of course, the 'bad guys'.

Answers to exercise b (page 26)

1a.   2c.   3d.   4d.   5b.   6b.   7b.   8a.
9c.   10a.

Follow-up work

Semi-controlled composition: Write a story (or an extract from a thriller) involving a car chase at night.

The text can be studied in combination with another piece of 'tough' narrative (for instance, 'Bat Dongin', page 28, or 'Gunfight in Pickering City', page 134), as a basis for a more ambitious piece of writing.

Practice unit 2.2

Bat Dongin

Note on the text

This text, and 'Gunfight in Pickering City' (page 134) are taken from a strange comedy western which ends with the Indians rescuing the white men from being massacred by the cavalry.

Answers to exercise a (page 29)

1c (or b?).   2d.   3c.   4a.   5b.   6b.   7a.
8a.   9d.   10c (or a or b?).

Follow-up work

This text is not particularly suitable as a basis for semi-controlled composition (because of its highly individual style), but could be studied in combination with another text to add some expressions and ideas (see follow-up work for 'A car chase', page 11 above).

Guidance on buying accessories

Answers to exercise b (page 31)

accessories: additional aids to motoring which can be fixed to a car.
rear screen heater: heater for the back window.
toddlers: small children.
untethered: not wearing safety belts.
pressure gauge: device for measuring air pressure in a tyre.
Wipac do one: the firm called 'Wipac' make a battery charger.
tow-rope: rope for pulling cars, etc.
roof-rack: frame that can be fixed on the roof for carrying luggage, etc.
boot racks: frames that can be fitted on top of the boot (luggage compartment at the back of the car) for carrying extra luggage.
touch-up paint: paint for covering scratches, etc.
car door buffers: rubber pieces which can be fixed on the outside of car doors to prevent them from being damaged by banging against walls, other cars' doors, etc.
lodged in crevices: stuck in small cracks or corners.

Follow-up work

Semi-controlled composition: What accessories would you buy for your car? Why?

Practice unit 2.3

Pitying animals

Note on the text

The famous Austrian scientist Konrad Lorenz was one of the founders of the systematic study of animal behaviour (ethology).

Answers to exercise (page 32)

1a.	2c.	3b.	4d.	5d.	6a.	7c.	8b.
9b.	10d.	11d.	12c.	13d.	14a.	15b.
16b.	17c.	18c.	19b.	20c.			

Follow-up work

Semi-controlled composition: What do you think about keeping animals in zoos? *Or*: Imagine you are an animal kept in captivity. Write about your experiences and feelings.
Class discussion on keeping animals in zoos.

Teaching unit 3: Understanding complicated sentences 1

Answers to exercise a (page 35)

1a. 2a. 3 One way (of deciding . . .). 4 Our holiday turned out to be satisfactory. 5 Arthur. 6 His father.
7 No. 8a.

Answers to exercise b (page 37)

1c. 2b. 3 The film. 4 Some soldiers. 5 A number of the children.

Practice unit 3.1

Invalid tricycles

Note on the text

The irony of the phrase 'all too clearly' (line 53) is probably unconscious.

Answers to exercise a (page 39)

1b. 2d. 3d (or c). 4b. 5a. 6c. 7b.
8c. 9c. 10c. 11b. 12b (or c) (the last *it* can refer either to the Department of Health's 'acting otherwise' or to the Department of Health itself).

Answers to exercise b (page 41)

1D. 2S. 3D. 4D. 5S. 6D (it was not the Consumers' Association that carried out the tests). 7D.
8S. 9S. 10D.

Practice unit 3.2

The workhouse

Answers to exercise a (page 42)

1c.   2a.   3d (and a).   4d.   5b.   6b.   7a.
8b (or d).   9d.   10c.

Follow-up work

Free composition or discussion: What do you think about people who don't work? Is it generally because they can't get work, or because they don't want to work?

Sleep

Answers to exercise b (page 44)

1c.   2d.   3b.   4c (or d?).   5d.   6a.   7a.
8c.   9b.   10a.

Teaching unit 4: Understanding complicated sentences 2

Answers to exercise a (page 46)

1   No – he may not offer himself as a candidate.
2   No.
3   Yes.
4   No – I told him I wanted to go.
5   Conversations about herself.

Answers to exercise b (page 47)

1   George insisted . . . if he had been invited.
2   If I were given . . .
3   She explained that as soon as she had closed the door (or: . . . just after she had closed the door), because of the draught, a terrible rattling noise was heard.
4   I could only tell you all my plans if I trusted you completely.

Letter to 'Time out'

Note on the text

Time Out is a weekly magazine which provides information about, and reviews of, films, concerts, plays and other entertainments in London.

Practice unit 4.1

 Notes on the great Mozart mystery

Note on the text

Bernard Levin writes regularly for *The Times*, mainly on politi-

16

cal and artistic matters. He is a self-conscious and often pompous stylist who writes some of the longest sentences in British journalism. However, he is also capable of brilliant satire, and can be passionate and moving when he feels strongly about something.

Answers to exercise (page 49)

1a.	2c.	3c.	4d.	5a.	6b.	7b.	8c.
9d.	10c.	11b.	12d.	13a.	14a.	15b (or c).	
16d.	17c.	18d.	19a.	20b.			

Section B:
Open-ended tests and summary-writing

Teaching unit 5: Open-ended tests

The bohemian marihuana smoker

Note on the text

This is taken from an essay in the Penguin book *Images of Deviance*.

Answers to exercise (page 57)

1   The police prefer quiet 'respectable' clothing; the marihuana smoker prefers bright expressive dress.
2   The police regard work as morally good; marihuana smokers don't.
3   He attacks the basic principles by which the policeman lives and understands his world.
4   American police officers.
5   They thought that drug users were a danger to the moral standards of society.
6   Marihuana users.
7   It's strange.
8   A policeman.
9   A marihuana smoker.
10   In theory.
11   Policemen can easily pick out marihuana smokers (and are provoked by their unconventional appearance).
12   No.
13   Negroes and drug users are both easily identified on sight.
14   Notting Hill is a working-class area: there are more police-men around than in a middle-class area, and marihuana smokers no longer have their families to protect them from police attention.
15   The police feel that other kinds of criminal share most of their attitudes to society, but that drug users disagree with these attitudes.

Follow-up work

Semi-controlled composition: How do you feel about the police attitude to drug users, as described in the text? Are you more in sympathy with bohemian values or traditional social attitudes to life?

Class discussion: Do you feel that marihuana smoking should be legalised? What about other kinds of drug use?

Role-playing: One member of the class is a journalist. Others are drug-users, parents and police. The journalist interviews the others. (Can be done as a TV programme.)

This text can usefully be studied in connection with 'Legalising pot' (page 127).

Practice unit 5.1

Washoe

Answers to exercise (page 58)

1 Viki only learnt four words; Washoe learnt thirty-four words, and could combine them into sentences.
2 The Hayes tried to teach Viki to speak (which is physically difficult for chimpanzees); Washoe was taught sign language.
3 The situation stayed the same; nothing changed.
4 Because a chimpanzee does not have the same physical difficulty in making signs as in trying to make speech sounds.
5 The symbols (or signs).
6 They took turns to work with her.
7 The experimenters (the Gardners and their colleagues).
8 Because children learn a lot of language from observing adults talking together.
9 In the right situation.
10 To make sure that the observation was correct.
11 Yes – dolphins.
12 To express correctly what she wanted to say.
13 She put signs together to make sentences.
14 A child knows far more words and makes longer sentences.

15 Because a three-year-old chimpanzee is as mature as a five-year-old child.
16 About three years.

Follow-up work

Semi-controlled composition: Washoe learns to read and write. Write a page or two from her diary.
Class discussion: What kind of intelligence do you think cats, dogs and other animals have?

Practice unit 5.2

 I love my lawyer

Note on the text

Eldridge Cleaver (like George Jackson and Malcolm X) was a leader of 'Black Consciousness' who educated himself by reading and discussion while in prison. His book *Soul on Ice*, a brilliantly-written series of essays on the situation of blacks in the United States, became a best-seller and made him famous. Cleaver has recently returned to the States after some years in exile in Algeria and elsewhere.

Answers to exercise (page 60)

1 They think he has no right to express himself because he's an uneducated black criminal.
2 No higher education.
3 By not keeping quiet, as they expect, and by not showing that he's sorry for what he's done.
4 Because he feels other people are as criminal as he is (due to their support for the Vietnam war).
5 Even though I'm a criminal, I don't owe any debt to a society which is responsible for the Vietnam war.
6 The Vietnamese people.
7 Because prisoners don't normally trust their lawyers.
8 For having some forbidden magazines (given him by his lawyer).
9 They thought the lawyer had done it on purpose to get him into trouble.

10   My lawyer had deliberately tried to get me into trouble.
11   A fool.
12   Because people usually let them down.
13   Prison life (the treatment prisoners receive).
14   Prison.
15   A prisoner.
16   Cynical and treacherous.
17   Treated with suspicion; used.

Follow-up work

Free composition: Cleaver was in prison for rape. Do you agree
with him that he didn't need to feel guilty because 'the blood of
Vietnamese peasants has paid off all my debts'?
Class discussion on the same subject.

Practice unit 5.3

Education: a father's experience

Mr Lucas uses some Yorkshire dialect forms. Note particularly
the second person singular pronoun and verb in 'Dost tha see it?'
(line 14).

Answers to exercise (page 62)

1   Mr Lucas and his wife.
2   Because for her, battles are not an important part of history.
3   Because he finds it fascinating.
4   This is a privilege given to people who have worked for the
     bus company for a long time.
5   When his children went to school.
6   Thousands of years ago, that part of the country was by
     the sea.
7   The way landscapes change.
8   That sort of information (the history of the earth and rocks:
     geology).
9   The cathedral.
10   The existence and work of Benjamin Britten.
11   He tried out the opera with some college students.
12   He put on the first performance of his opera.
13   Music.

14 Archaeologists.
15 The artists made them so that they would last for a long time.
16 You start thinking about how civilisations pass.
17 To awaken his interest in a lot of things he had never thought about before.
18 History, geology, architecture, music, archaeology.

Follow-up work

Free composition: Do you know anyone who has had a similar experience to that of Mr Lucas or his daughter? Did your education have any effect on your family?
Talks on the same subject.

Teaching unit 6: Introduction to summary

Answers to exercise a (page 63)

1   George smokes.
2   Mary worked well.
3   My sister likes older people.
4   Most foreigners find English pronunciation difficult.
5   I've stopped believing in Father Christmas.
6   The British drink a lot of tea.
7   Some long and complicated sentences mean very little.
8   Big cities have growing traffic problems.
9   'To be or not to be, that is the question.'

Adolescent students

Answer to exercise b (page 63)

c.

Follow-up work

Semi-controlled composition: Write about *either* an adolescent you know *or* another stage of life (childhood or old age, for instance).
Class discussion: Do you think what the writer says about adolescents is true?

Violence

Note on the text

Krishnamurti is an Indian philosopher.

Answer to exercise c (page 64)

Look at the violence outside and inside yourself without judging, without justifying or condemning it.

Follow-up work

Class discussion: What exactly is Krishnamurti trying to say about anger, and how to deal with it? Do you find his ideas sensible?

The Clark–Trimble experiments

Note on the text

Paul Jennings is a well-known humorous writer. This passage is a good example of typically British humour, both because of the subject-matter (the writer is laughing, basically, at his own clumsiness), and because of the treatment (the humour relies on the contrast between the serious academic style and the absurd content). See also 'Twenty joke menthols, please' (page 106).

Answers to exercise d (page 65)

1   The more expensive the carpet, the more often toast falls marmalade-side down on it.
2   To amuse the reader.

Gun control

Note on the text

Readers will no doubt be struck by the extreme confusion of thought and its reflection in the style.

Answers to exercise e (page 66)

Gun-owners are good citizens, and everyone should be free to own guns; if we wish to reduce crime, we should not ban guns, but impose harsher punishments for criminals.

Follow-up work

Free composition or discussion: Do you think ordinary citizens should have the right to carry guns, as they do in the United States?

Practice unit 6.1

Freedom and selfishness

Answers to exercise (page 68)

1 Concern with one's own personal needs is not selfish — it's necessary to understand oneself before one can be useful to others.
2 We can't make things happen just by wishing.
3 People don't know how to use freedom: it has to be learnt.
4 We've learnt to do what other people want us to do, so we aren't used to freedom.
5 Freedom.
6 The authority of others.
7 When you've finished doing all the things you first want to do.
8 Doing all the things you thought you never had the chance to do.
9 Make your life meaningful.
10 Authority.
11 He is hostile to Christianity, which he thinks stops people concentrating on their real needs.
12 The idea that you should think of others, not yourself.
13 Thinking of other people instead of oneself.
14 Because Americans have learnt to put the needs of society before their own needs, society has become very powerful and authoritarian.
15 Because the writer doesn't think that it is really good.
16 Questions which suggest one is selfish.
17 To make ourselves feel valuable and important, and to be like other people.

Follow-up work

Free composition or discussion: What do you think about the writer's attitudes?

Practice unit 6.2

Teaching speech
Received Pronunciation

Note on the texts

In Britain, and particularly in England, people's speech (especially their pronunciation) has traditionally been regarded as an indication of their social class.

Answers to exercise a (page 69)

1   The way we learn our language, and the way we are taught to think about it.
2   People are not sure what is meant by 'good speech'.
3   To make people speak in an Americanised way, and to reduce the tendency to imitate 'public-school' English.
4   Public-school (or upper-class) English.
5   The fact that schools and teachers tell people that their language is wrong or inferior.
6   Speech training.
7   The upper class.
8   A situation in which people speak one form of the language but are taught that a different form is correct.
9   In other social classes.
10 No.
11 Speech-training that suggests that one form of a language is better than others.
12 It makes people feel inferior and resentful, and makes them reject quality (in cultural matters) because it is associated with a social class that they do not belong to.

Answers to exercise b (page 70)

1   A standard pronunciation in Britain.
2   Pronunciation is variable (even among educated speakers), and 'Received Pronunciation' has lost a lot of its prestige.
3   Pronunciation and handwriting are both variable, so that each person has his own.
4   Handwriting and pronunciation.
5   And other regional accents.
6   It is becoming less respected.

Follow-up work

Semi-controlled composition: In Britain, one form of the language is considered 'correct' and others are often regarded as 'incorrect'. Is there a similar situation in your country? If so, what do you feel about it?
Class discussion: Should people be able to speak and write as they like? If not, why not?

Practice unit 6.3

 ### Sex and the Party

Note on the text

George Orwell's famous novel *1984* presents a terrifying picture of an imaginary totalitarian state in which everybody's behaviour, including his thoughts, is controlled by the authorities. The book was inspired by the dictatorships of the 1930s.

Answers to exercise (page 72)

1   The Party did not want people to escape into a private world through sex; it wanted to transform sexual energy into enthusiasm for the leader and for war.
2   It seemed strange that Julia should already know these things.
3   Because she had known plenty of people like her, and had had the same education as her.
4   No.
5   Marriage with Katharine.
6   The fact that Katharine called sex 'our duty to the Party'.
7   She means 'as well as Katharine' — they had had the same sort of education.
8   The indoctrination about sex that Julia is talking about.
9   Whether people really believe what they are taught or not.
10   Her way of expressing this idea.
11   The Party leaders.
12   The Party had found a way of using it for their own purposes.
13   Because it created a private world outside the Party's control.

14   She thought it was stupid.
15   The Party's use of children as spies.
16   The Party encouraged parents to love their children, but taught children to spy on their parents.
17   Children.

Follow-up work

Free composition: Do you agree with Orwell's idea that totalitarian regimes discourage sexual pleasure because it creates a world outside their control?

Teaching unit 7: Writing summaries

 ## Progress in Samoa

Answer to exercise (page 74)

The country is rapidly being modernised. Improvements include new roads, an up-to-date communications system, a big new tourist hotel, a radio station and a sawmill. These changes are bringing foreign investors and advisers flooding into Samoa, and European-style houses are appearing everywhere. On the other hand, many young Samoans are leaving for New Zealand. The money they send home is changing the country's economy, causing neglect of agriculture and inflation. Economic changes seem likely to be followed by political changes.

Follow-up work

Semi-controlled composition: Write about a place you know which is being modernised in the same way as Samoa.
Class discussion: Do you think this kind of progress is basically a good or a bad thing?

Practice unit 7.1

 ## The new music

Note on the text

In *The Greening of America*, Charles Reich enthusiastically supports the protest movements of the 1960s, and the changes in music, dress and life-styles that accompanied them. He felt that these developments marked the beginning of a cultural revolution which would change capitalist society out of all recognition.

Answers to exercise (page 75)

1   Folk music, blues and rock.
2   They expressed the attitudes and way of life of three differ-
     ent social groups.
3   The three forms of music.
4   New ways of experiencing one's surroundings, and new atti-
     tudes to the world.
5   Things changed by themselves without outside influence.
6   The change.
7   The Beatles and some San Francisco rock groups.
8   Before 1967, white blues musicians imitated blacks; after,
     they made the music their own.
9   The blues.
10   The three different forms of music were brought together.
11   The sound of non-electric instruments.
12   Sounded as if they had a supernatural origin.
13   They made possible new sounds, new recording tricks, and
     much greater volume.
14   The audience felt as if they were part of the music.
15   The experience of listening (and dancing) to music accom-
     panied by lighting effects.
16   Three separate kinds of music (folk, rock and blues) were
     brought together, and influences from other traditions (e.g.
     Indian) were added, to make a much more complex sort of
     music expressing new attitudes. Electronic devices were
     used to give music a new sound: it became much louder,
     and was associated with lighting effects. This (and the use
     of drugs) made the audience feel that they were not just
     listening passively, but participating in a 'total experience'.

Follow-up work

Semi-controlled composition: Do you like any of the kinds of
music described in the text? If so, what kinds?

Practice unit 7.2

Lie detector

Answers to exercise (page 77)

1   No — apparently it shows nervous stress.

2　Testing people to see if they are suitable for jobs.

3　Some muscles tighten and stop vibrating – this changes the sound of the voice.

4　Burns are using one of the machines; Dektor are the manufacturers.

5　No – just one low-frequency part of the sound.

6　To show what a person's voice sounds like when there is no stress, and when he is lying.

7　By assuming without proof that a person who shows stress is lying.

8　Going at the speed he wants.

9　By tape-recording his answers and analysing the recording afterwards.

10　Because a person may show stress because he is unhappy about the loss of (or damage to) a valued possession.

11　An approach that may be wrong.

12　The writer wants to show that he does not know whether the claim is justified.

13　Less money than he asked for.

14　It's very worrying that the PSE might be used in Britain.

15　Because (in the writer's opinion) the machine will first of all be used in harmless-looking situations, but later (when people are used to it) for more sinister purposes of an anti-democratic kind.

16　According to the manufacturers, the machine can help both police and private industry to investigate people's honesty. Firms use it to test applicants for jobs (for instance, to check on drug use or political attitudes), and to see whether their staff are honest. Insurance investigators use it to detect false claims, and to see whether clients will accept less money than they should get. There are three main objections: the machine only detects stress (which may not be due to dishonesty); it could be used for political control; and its accuracy depends on the skill of the operator.

Practice unit 7.3

 Dilemma of the working mother

Answers to exercise (page 79)

1　Because happy children are easier to deal with.

2 The most important decision.
3 Doctor Spock has the normal orthodox attitude.
4 The attention a mother can give her child.
5 She thinks it is too simple.
6 Loving care and stimulation.
7 Because they may be too depressed or worn out by the repetitive work of looking after a child to give it proper attention.
8 She can buy labour-saving machines (which free her from routine housework), and she can pay for a better environment for her child.
9 The fact that they are trapped at home doing boring work.
10 Starting a career from the beginning again.
11 The arrangement.
12 A free day.
13 Get to know them well before leaving.
14 Children don't like their mother giving all her attention to a job.
15 The expression suggests that if a mother is depressed she can't pay proper attention to her child.
16 The boring routine work involved in bringing up small children can cause depression, and it is important for a mother to find ways of escaping from this. One solution is to work, and pay someone else to look after the children during the day. Women who do not go out to work can arrange for someone to look after the children once a week, so that they can have a completely free day and perhaps an evening out with their husbands. Weekends without the children (perhaps organised by means of a family exchange) are also a good idea.

Follow-up work

Semi-controlled composition: Do you agree with the writer of the article that it might be a good idea for a mother of small children to go out to work?
Class discussion on the same subject.

Practice unit 7.4

Rescue archaeology in Scotland

Answers to exercise (page 81)

1   Because machines used for building are destroying traces of the past.
2   Disturbingly fast.
3   The threatened towns.
4   Because there are few written records dating from before the seventeenth century.
5   Rescue.
6   Scotland.
7   In Scottish towns.
8   The inhabitants of Scottish towns.
9   Information about people's lives, diet, health, and social habits, about their patterns of trade, and about their houses, churches and defences.
10   A very small proportion of it is given to Scotland.
11   Five towns.
12   Lack of money and trained archaeologists.
13   There are very few archaeologists who have the training necessary to organise quick investigations in places where building work is going to be carried out.
14   Rescue.
15   The things that can be found out by archaeological study of buried remains.
16   Archaeological evidence.
17   Change is no longer slow.
18   Scottish rescue archaeology has a difficult task, because sites (particularly in towns) are being redeveloped very fast, and information is being lost for ever. At the same time, there is a shortage of money and trained staff. One suggestion is that twenty archaeologists should be employed to work with local government bodies so as to improve communication between local authorities and developers. An archaeological study is going to be made at Perth (the site of the old Scottish parliament), before redevelopment takes place. It is important, too, to make the public aware of the situation.

Practice unit 7.5

The causes of conflict

Answers to exercise (page 83)

1 To find out more about the causes of aggression and fight-ing.
2 Other children or apes.
3 Things which more than one person wanted.
4 The person who fights to get something is himself killed.
5 The thing that is fought for.
6 Toys and other objects.
7 It is a form of possessiveness (the first cause mentioned).
8 The 'object of desire' is the thing desired.
9 Difference from other members of the same race or type of animal.
10 Interesting new things like animals.
11 Inability to do what they want to do.
12 The thing that is attacked.
13 No.
14 The fact that people take revenge on innocent objects.
15 Because it helps to explain why fighting and wars take place.
16 To understand the causes of conflict.
17 The author found three main causes of fighting among apes and children. The first was the desire for possession: the resulting fighting could lead to the destruction of the toy or animal desired. Among children, a possession might be valued (and fought for) only when another child wanted it. Jealousy is a form of possessiveness. A second cause was aggression against a strange child or animal (but not against a member of another species). And finally, frustration can lead to aggression against a totally innocent object or per-son; the author sees this as an important cause of conflict.

Follow-up work

Semi-controlled composition: Do you agree with the writer's ideas about the causes of conflict? Can you give any examples from your own experience?
Class discussion: Can you think of any ways in which we might be able to make war less likely?

Section C:
Perception of the effective use of English

Teaching unit 8: Appreciation of a writer's use of language 1

Firm friends of ours

Note on the text

Michael Frayn first made his reputation as a satirical humorist with short pieces of this kind in *The Guardian* and *The Observer*. Later he went on to write novels and plays.

Answers to exercise (page 87)

1b (he means that the Crumbles have an annoying habit of giving other people advice about all sorts of things).   2a, b, d, e, h.
3c.   4d (perhaps to make the Crumbles appear not only affected, but also united against the writer and his wife).   5c.
6a.
7   ' . . . it seems very surprising that you haven't bought one yet.'
8   To exaggerate the idea that the Crumbles are very knowledgeable, so as to make them sound ridiculous.
9   To make the Crumbles sound united against the writer and his wife.
10   The idea of competition at the pre-nursery school level is completely absurd, but illustrates (by exaggeration) the competitive attitudes that many middle-class parents have towards their children's education.
11   No.
12   It also reminds one that the Crumbles are laying down the law about a subject they know nothing about.
13b.

Practice unit 8.1

🔲 **Traveller's tales**

Note on the text

See note on 'Firm friends of ours', page 35 above.

Answers to exercise (page 91)

1   'particularly helpful' (line 8); 'did I come across a social
    pressure?' (line 16); 'we met the wrong lot of housewives'
    (line 28); 'Bitterly regret . . . ' (line 35); 'totally failed to
    get themselves branded as communists' (line 37); 'by some
    unfortunate local atypicality' (line 47); 'we met the wrong
    lot of American children too' (line 49); 'which just goes to
    show the dangers . . . ' (line 50); 'Particularly since it turns
    out to be so much like they'd always supposed' (lines 54—5).

2   Christopher and Lavinia interrupt people.

3   Everybody else's.

4   Lavinia.

5   The use of 'must' shows the Crumbles' confidence in their
    opinions about places they have never been to.

6   He is pretending to suggest that the Crumbles have cor-
    rected his picture of America. In fact, of course, this is an
    ironic way of showing how dogmatic and pretentious the
    Crumbles are.

7   Here, the writer shows how the Crumbles (who have done
    all the talking) have, not surprisingly, had their opinion of
    America confirmed.

8   To amuse the reader by satirising a particular type of per-
    son.

Follow-up work

Semi-controlled composition: Write an imaginary conversation
between yourself and some foreigners who have never been to
your country but who think they know all about it.

Practice unit 8.2

 ### The fish dream

Note on the text

In *Catch-22*, Joseph Heller uses the absurdity of war as a symbol of the much greater absurdity which he sees in the world as a whole.

Answers to exercise (page 93)

1   He felt (or was trying to feel) superior to Yossarian.
2   He hoped that Yossarian would say that the fish reminded him of something interesting.
3   He was being friendly to Yossarian but didn't really feel warm towards him.
4   Yossarian was using psychiatrists' language, and so Major Sanderson felt that he had found someone he had something in common with.
5   To show a contrast with what he had expected – most people don't understand.
6   Major Sanderson wants to talk about sex: he feels that this is the real purpose of the conversation.
7   To show that Major Sanderson's excitement is making him speak very quickly.
8   It satirises Major Sanderson's feeling that fish are symbolic of sex, by suggesting the opposite; it probably upsets Major Sanderson (by making him feel ridiculed), and is obviously meant to amuse the reader.
9   To amuse the reader by satirising a certain kind of psychiatrist.

Follow-up work

Semi-controlled composition: Write an imaginary interview between someone you know (for example, a friend, your teacher, yourself) and a psychiatrist.

Practice unit 8.3

 ### The painter

Note on the text

This is taken from a short story, set in Paris after the First World War, at a time when a lot of Americans went there to study art.

Answers to exercise (page 94)

1   d.
2   One of the painters (the narrator and her friends) whose attitudes are shown in the text.
3   It is a dramatic and exaggerated form of expression.
4   This is an unusual (and therefore more vivid) way of saying 'go out blushing'.
5   To suggest the slow, purposeless way of moving of people who have plenty of spare time.
6   'you'; 'too thrilling for words'; 'the most awful gloom'; 'my dear, yes'; 'that ragtime thing'.
7   Women artists who were interested in the boy.
8   One artist to another.
9   b.

Teaching unit 9: Appreciation of a writer's use of language 2

Danny
The old man

Note on the texts

Although Steinbeck and Hemingway have very different ways of writing, it is worth noting that they both use stylistic tricks to spread a sort of romantic glow over their characters.

Answers to exercise a (page 96)

1   The repetitions ('of', 'and of', 'and of'; 'Danny', 'Danny's', 'Danny's') make the sentence sound rhythmical and impressive.
2   'Speak of' is a rather old-fashioned, uncommon way of saying 'talk about'. It reminds the reader of the language of classical literature, and so makes the passage sound more glamorous or impressive.
3   To make Danny and his friends sound romantic.
4   The unusual word-order is characteristic of romantic poetry.
5   'Endeavours' is a more literary, impressive word.
6   Most of the sentences are built up of two or three similar parts, often involving repetition of key-words; this gives a musical, rhythmical sound to the style.

Answers to exercise b (page 97)

1   Not to talk unnecessarily.
2   The sequence of tenses ('. . . that I *am* crazy') is abnormal in English, and gives the impression of a foreigner talking.
3   It's strange to say that radios 'talk' to people: this makes the reader feel, perhaps, that the old man is a simple person who has little experience of radios or other aspects of civilisation.

4   The language here is very literary. 'Since' (in the sense of
     'because') is unusual in spoken English, and a speaker would
     normally use contractions ('I'm' instead of 'I am'). This per-
     haps makes the old man sound more impressive.
5   'That which' is a very unusual, old-fashioned, literary (and
     therefore impressive) way of saying 'what' or 'the thing
     which'.
6   To give him prestige and importance by making him sound
     not only simple but also strange and exotic (like people in
     old stories).
7   Steinbeck repeats content-words, like nouns, names, verbs
     and adjectives: the effect is to make his characters sound
     important and romantic. Hemingway repeats form-words
     (pronouns and conjunctions), and the effect is one of
     monotony, which helps to create the impression that a
     fisherman's life is hard, boring and repetitive.

Follow-up work

Stylistic exercise: an amusing exercise for advanced students is
to try to rewrite one passage in the style of the other ('This is
the story of the old man and the old man's boat and the old
man's sea . . . ').

Practice unit 9.1

 Memories of childhood

Note on the text

Dylan Thomas is best known for his poetry and for his radio
play *Under Milk Wood*, set in Wales, where he grew up. He has a
very individual style: a critic once said that Thomas used words
as if he were present at their creation.

Answers to exercise (page 98)

1   These are vivid and unusual comparisons.
2   Again, this is an unusual and striking description — it forces
     the thinness of the pier's legs on the reader's attention.
3   He means that the museum was old, dusty and boring.

4   It was a simplified version of cricket; when we played we scratched on the hard ground with sticks.

5   Eyes looking towards the sea. By inventing a new word, the writer helps to make his prose more vivid and personal, and to make a striking impression on the reader.

6   The children (who had paid threepence to see the film) shouted and hissed to show what they felt about the characters on the screen.

7   The answer to this question depends on one's definition of 'poetic style'. There are a number of features of Dylan Thomas's writing which are more common in poetry than in prose. In particular: unusual word-order and sentence-structure ('bent and Devon-facing sea-shore'; 'the inexhaustible and mysterious, bushy Red-Indian hiding park'; 'the sometimes tearful wicked'); alliteration ('wander whistling'; 'stale as station sandwiches'); elliptical descriptions ('the groves were blue with sailors'); unusual comparisons ('skeleton legs', etc.).

8   To portray, in romanticised form, some of his childhood memories.

Follow-up work

Free composition: Write some of your own childhood memories.

Practice unit 9.2

 Puma humour

Note on the text

The humorous treatment of the subject (and the clever title) are typical of *The Guardian*'s approach to less serious news items.

Answers to exercise (page 99)

1   To imitate the style of a speaker telling a story.
2   The heavy formal style creates a humorous effect.
3   To restrain the puma.
4   A humorous effect, resulting from the incongruity of the comparison of the inside of the car with a jungle.

5   To make a joke. Broken-down cars are towed – it sounds
     funny to use the word for a drunk man.
6   The expression is used to make a humorous contrast with
     the puma's owner, who was charged with being 'drunk and
     incapable'.
7   This, again, is humorous (because of the absurdity of the
     idea that a puma could appreciate the atmosphere of a pub).
8   In these two paragraphs the writer drops his humorous style
     for a short time and simply reports the facts.

Practice unit 9.3

Science and maths graduates

Answers to exercise a (page 100)

1   To inform potential maths and science teachers of the qual-
     ities needed for successful teaching, and to persuade them to
     go in for this career.
2   The words chosen to list the qualities needed in a teacher
     ('patience', 'understanding', 'tact', etc.) make the profession
     sound glamorous and challenging.
3   The rhythm of the first part ('If you have a desire . . . ') is
     repeated in the second ('if you have patience . . . '); this
     creates a musical and persuasive effect.

The great escape

Answers to exercise b (page 101)

1   To persuade people to go on a cruise on one of the adver-
     tiser's ships.
2   The first text has complex sentence-structure, a rhythmical
     and balanced style, and vocabulary that is basically infor-
     mative (even though it is designed to persuade at the same
     time). In the second text, most of the sentences are very
     short and simple; many of them are broken up by a full
     stop so that each part can strike the reader with more force
     (e.g. ' . . . band of fellow voyagers. Instead of being . . . ').
     To heighten this effect, there are very frequent paragraph
     divisions. There is some repetition (for instance, 'you'll . . . '
     in lines 14–18). A great deal of the vocabulary is chosen so

as to persuade rather than inform: examples are 'a lucky
few', 'really get away from it all', 'exclusive', 'rare oppor-
tunity', 'very select band', 'impressive', 'splendid', 'spec-
tacular', 'leisurely'.

⊞ What energy crisis?

Answers to exercise c (page 101)

1 It is directed at the general public, and intended to persuade them to save energy.
2 The chatty, conversational style is typical of a lot of adver-
   tising: the use of contractions ('There's') and spoken structures ('Funny sort of crisis') are supposed to make the
   reader feel he is being talked to. The very short sentences,
   and the use of slang ('costing a bomb') are designed to make
   a complicated subject easy to understand.

Follow-up work

Semi-controlled composition: Write a job advertisement, a travel
advertisement, and a government announcement encouraging
people to save something (for instance, water).

Section D:
Practice tests

Practice test 1

 ### Conversation at breakfast

Note on the text

This is from Keith Waterhouse's best-known novel, *Billy Liar*, which was made into a successful film. The author writes regularly for the *Daily Mirror*.

Answers to exercise (page 106)

1   To suggest that Billy's mother shouted very loudly, and perhaps that she repeated the same cries every day.
2   They are both threats.
3   This is an amusing way of saying that the family were not usually talking when Billy came down to breakfast.
4   The conversation based on Billy's mother's attempts to get him up.
5   Normal replies to this remark.
6   To be sarcastic – he felt that his father's remark was so obvious that it wasn't worth making.
7   If the egg was cold it must already be a quarter to nine.
8   A commonly used stock remark.
9   His father.
10   It makes Gran's dress sound more elegant and formal.
11   'He wants to burn' (= he needs to burn); 'of a morning' (= in the morning).
12   If she wanted to talk to somebody and there was nobody else in the room to go through.
13   The writer's approach is to use satire and caricature to make the family sound ridiculous.

Practice test 2

 Twenty joke menthols, please

Note on the text

Another example of Paul Jennings laughing gently at his own weaknesses. See note on 'The Clark–Trimble experiments', page 24 above.

Answers to exercise (page 108)

1   The style is very literary, both because of the structure (with the repetitions of 'I shall') and the vocabulary ('calm', 'sunny plateau', 'vast meaningful harmony', 'holy content'). The effect is to suggest that his view of the future is exaggeratedly optimistic, and so to laugh at himself.
2   The busy (hectic) period.
3   This is ironic – he knows it isn't the last packet.
4   These are other occasions when an important experience has come to an end.
5   ' . . . but now we have to say goodbye.'
6   The writer suggests that when he thinks he is giving up smoking he is a little like a lunatic who thinks that he is a poached egg.
7   To stress the paradoxical fact that his attempts to cut down smoking are making him spend more money, not less.
8   His non-smoking aids.
9   This is ironic – he is, of course, a smoker.
10 The first part of the sentence has a slightly literary flavour; the last five words are much more down to earth, and the contrast creates a humorous effect.
11 Cigarettes rolled in the cigarette machine.
12 To amuse the reader.

Practice test 3

 Lord Moping

Note on the text

Evelyn Waugh is best known as the author of several well-known novels (for instance, *Decline and Fall, Brideshead Revisited*). *Mr Loveday's Little Outing* is a brilliant short story with a surprise ending.

Answers to exercise (page 109)

1   Lady Moping speaks in a very formal, non-conversational way. Her style is like that of written English: examples are 'will not' (instead of 'won't'); 'greatly changed'.

2   The style reflects the confused, eventful afternoon that is described, and serves to distinguish this reference to the past from the rest of the passage.

3   The writer seems to be suggesting that the upper classes can take it for granted that they will receive special privileges.

4   The wealthier lunatics.

5   The asylum.

6   This suggests that no attempt was made, in the address, to hide the fact that it was a hospital for mad people.

7   Gave the impression that working-class lunatics might be found there.

8   The first expression says more or less directly what sort of institution is involved; the second is euphemistic — there is an attempt to make mental illness sound less distressing.

9   He had caused a scandal on an occasion which was very important to Lady Moping's pursuit of social success.

Practice test 4

 At these prices, who can afford not to?

Note on the text

Abbie Hoffman was one of the more colourful figures of the American student protest movement of the 1960s. The book from which this text is taken is a half-serious course in how to live outside the rules and laws of society.

Answers to exercise (page 110)

1   'These prices' are not prices at all: the writer is talking about ways of getting things free.

2   They are hidden under the shopper's clothes.

3   This is a humorous use of the language of religious people.
4   What you ask for.
5   The officials in the station lost property office.
6   The method just explained.
7   Nice, or good-quality.
8   This is an amusing and striking way of saying 'wear clothes that nobody will notice or remember'.
9   There are a large number of short sentences, with many imperative structures. The style is conversational and often slangy.
10 To suggest, in an amusing way, how people can get things without paying for them.

Follow-up work

Free composition or discussion: What do you feel about the writer's attitude to life?

Practice test 5

Left holding the baby

Answers to exercise (page 112)

1b.   2c.   3c.   4d.   5d.   6a.   7b.   8c.
9c.   10a.

Submarine rescue

Answers to exercise (page 114)

1c.   2d (or a).   3d.   4a.   5a.   6a.   7d.
8c.   9c.   10b.

Follow-up work

Semi-controlled composition: Imagine you are one of the men who were trapped in the submarine, and write your account of what happened.

Practice test 6

Perception

Answers to exercise (page 116)

1d. 2c. 3d. 4a. 5a. 6c. 7b. 8a.
9c. 10c. 11d.

Margo and Peter

Note on the text

Gerald Durrell is a well-known zoologist who writes humorous books about his experiences collecting animals in various parts of the world. He is the brother of Lawrence Durrell, the novelist.

Answers to exercise (page 118)

1b. 2c. 3c. 4d. 5c. 6a. 7c (or a).
8d. 9b.

Follow-up work

Semi-controlled or free composition: Write a story entitled 'My tragic love-story'.

Practice test 7

Gentle Ghost

Answers to exercise (page 121)

1d. 2a. 3c. 4c. 5b. 6d. 7b. 8a.
9c. 10c. 11d.

Ski-ing down Everest

Answers to exercise (page 123)

1d. 2a. 3b. 4b. 5c. 6d. 7c. 8a.
9b (or c?).

Practice test 8

Home-made atomic bomb

Answers to exercise (page 125)

1c.   2b.   3d.   4b.   5a.   6b.   7c.   8a.
9a.   10d.   11c.   12d.

Legalising pot

Answers to exercise (page 127)

1c.   2c.   3a.   4b.   5d.   6b.   7b.   8d.
9b.   10d.

Follow-up work

Semi-controlled composition: Say what you think about the arguments for and against legalising pot.
Class discussion on the same subject.

It may be useful to study this text in conjunction with 'The bohemian marihuana smoker' (page 56).

Practice test 9

A séance

Answers to exercise (page 130)

1   To show that the apparently supernatural things which happened at spiritualist séances could actually be produced by trickery.
2   Some of the impressive happenings which mediums used to produce.
3   To convince people that nobody could come in from outside during the séance.
4   The first witness said that the musical box floated about; he referred to knockings and bright lights; he mentioned that the man bowed, and disappeared with a scraping noise. The second witness did not include these details, but said

that the man had a beard and was reading a book; he added that at the end of the séance the door was still locked and sealed.

5   To stop him from doing anything to deceive the others.
6   He referred to a clammy hand, a bluish-white light, a frightful apparition, a mummy, and a bearded man of oriental appearance with a disturbing expression.
7   Thoroughly practised beforehand.
8   Pretended to lock the door.
9   Things which were used for the performance.
10   Because Mr Davey distracted their attention just when they were about to search the cupboard containing the props.
11   The prop-cupboard.
12   To search the cupboard.
13   Because he came into the room after the lights had been put out, and while the musical box was playing.
14   The paper seal on the door.
15   The performance.
16   A medium is someone who communicates with the dead; a conjuror is a person who uses tricks to produce impossible-looking effects.
17   The witnesses thought the room was locked, and that they were alone with Mr Davey. They believed that they saw various supernatural phenomena, such as the spirits of a man and a woman, accompanied by strange lights and noises. In fact, the door was not locked, and the effects were produced by a colleague of Mr Davey who came into the room under cover of darkness and the noise of the musical box. He used materials which had been hidden in a cupboard that was not searched because Mr Davey distracted people's attention at a crucial moment.

Practice test 10

The biggest flying monster in the world
Monster could not flap wings

Answers to exercise (page 132)

1   The creature whose remains have been found was much bigger than all other known flying reptiles.
2   They use the bones (and pieces of bone) that they have dis-

covered as a basis for calculating the size of the complete reptile.

3   To start up an old argument again.
4   He felt it was too big to be able to do this.
5   It was almost impossible to work out how it flew because we didn't know how heavy it was.
6   Species of flying reptiles.
7   The front legs were part of the wings.
8   It did not live near the sea (and possibly lived on carrion).
9   The layers of rock in which it was found did not originate under the sea.
10 The coat.
11 That the reptile had leathery wings without feathers.
12 The fact of being warm-blooded and furry.
13 Flying reptile.
14 A bigger flying reptile.
15 The latest discovery.
16 The remains of extinct flying reptiles have been found in Texas. The size of the bones suggests that they were much bigger than other known flying creatures. However, it is impossible to calculate their weight, and therefore to be sure how they flew; they may have been too big to flap their wings. Unlike most prehistoric reptiles, they did not live on fish (they were not found in ocean sediments) and possibly ate carrion. They are thought to have had feather-less, leathery wings, but one scientist believes they were warm-blooded and covered with fur.

Practice test 11

 Grammar school

Answers to exercise (page 134)

1   Children who already knew people at the grammar school.
2   The first weeks at grammar school.
3   I immediately settled down happily at Marburton College.
4   The place where they had grown up.
5   Because of their enthusiastic attitude to the new school, their first school exercises were good.
6   Difficult, challenging situations.
7   The middle-class world of the grammar school.

8   Working class.
9   The breakdown of home support.
10   She felt different from all the other children – she had come from a different world.
11   The working-class children.
12   The middle-class children.
13   Having a uniform that was too big.
14   To force them to fit into the system.
15   The fact that this treatment could cause problems.
16   Because everything was new and different.
17   Because their parents didn't understand the grammar school.
18   Most of the children lost their old friends and found themselves in a new and confusing world with people, rules, attitudes and subjects that were hard to understand. They met middle-class children who coped well with the system and made them feel inferior. In some schools the teachers treated them harshly for the first few weeks to make them conform, and this added to the confusion. Not all children could ask their families for help and advice, because working-class parents did not always understand the grammar school.

Follow-up work

Semi-controlled or free composition: Write about your own experience of starting a new school.

Practice test 12

Gunfight in Pickering City

Answers to exercise (page 136)

1   Because he hoped to make money both as a doctor and as a newspaper publisher.
2   Two.
3   They were drunk.
4   In the saloon.
5   They had not yet begun to learn multiplication at her school.
6   Alerting her father to the situation.
7   Coming to get shot.
8   He was drunk, and this affected his pronunciation.
9   Franklin Heller's gunbelt.

10   He was only wearing one boot.
11   A loaded gun on each hip.
12   They were wearing one gunbelt between them, and this
     held them close together.
13   He meant 'It doesn't matter'.
14   To attract her father's attention.
15   Evaliña hit the sheriff.
16   They were confused by Evaliña's shooting.
17   Evaliña.
18   Four gunmen started walking down the main street to kill
     Jim Street and Irish Reyes. Evaliña tried to warn them, but
     they had difficulty in concentrating because they were
     drunk. Finally they understood, and after trying to put on
     their boots, they went out to meet the gunmen, wearing
     one enormous gunbelt between them. Evaliña fired a shot
     through the bank window, alerting her father (and hitting
     the sheriff); her father jumped out through the window and
     killed the gunmen, who were distracted by Evaliña's shot.

Follow-up work

See follow-up work for 'Bat Dongin', page 12 above.